This book belongs to:

_____

From:

_____

Date:

_____

Message:

_____

_____

Copyright © 2018 by Christian Art Kids, an imprint of Christian Art Publishers,
PO Box 1599, Vereeniging, 1930, RSA

359 Longview Drive, Bloomingdale, IL 60108, USA

First edition 2018

Cover designed by Christian Art Publishers
Illustrations by Catherine Groenewald

Printed in China

ISBN 978-1-4321-2581-3

18 19 20 21 22 23 24 25 26 27 – 10 9 8 7 6 5 4 3 2 1

This book is dedicated to:

my beloved Arnold,

my precious children:
Michael, Jacqui, Duane,
Therina, Colette and Billy Bob,

and my awesome grandchildren:
Joshua, Jodi, Rachael, Kyra, Blaise, Leeza,
Levi, Naethan, Jasmine and Roxanna.

FOREWORD

I see my mother's love for child evangelism highlighted on every page of this book. She has been involved in Children's Ministry for over 50 years and has never lost the energy and zeal to engage the kids in her special way, and to touch their hearts.

What a privilege to have a mother who loves the Lord as deeply as she does, and emotionally connects with everyone around her to their benefit.

As the stories unfold through the pages of this book, she uses a mixture of real-life examples (true stories) and fiction to share a journey of spiritual lessons learned by the children. These are genuine life lessons that are valuable and precious for every child to hear in this day and age.

Mom's heartfelt writing is captivated in her emotional portrayal of events that draw the reader into each real-life situation as if they were present there themselves (it even takes the older generations back to those formative years).

This book not only serves as a precious collection of life's accounts for growing children, but is also well constructed as bedtime discussion pieces. It can also serve as family prayer "kick-starters" for the younger generation and parents alike.

I hope you will be enriched through reading this as much as I have had the privilege of being raised by my mother's words.

May our dear Lord get all the glory as children's lives are changed through this precious treat.

Dr. Duane Mol
ENT Surgeon

INTRODUCTION

Do you know what I as a grandmother enjoy about my grandchildren? It's the happy memories that we share and create together. I love my grandchildren, but God loves you even more. And you will learn about His love and care in the chapters that follow. So I am longing that you will find these special "treasures" that I have already found. Isn't that special? And that is why you are reading **Grammy's Treasure Chest.** A chest FULL of exciting treasures.

But I can just hear you asking, "How do I go about finding these treasures?" Well, here's the secret. Each evening, after supper, as you get together with Mom or Dad, ask them to read a chapter to you. At the end of each chapter you have to try and find out what the treasure is in the story. Ask Mom or Dad to give you a clue. There will be a different treasure in each chapter and each one answers the question: what would God love me to know?

There is also a prayer that you can pray and the end of each story, and a fun activity for you to do to remind you of the truth that you have just heard.

Then at the end of the book all the special treasures are listed. You can memorize them, one by one. See how clever you are and how many you can remember. Maybe Mom or Dad will even give you a prize. Who knows? But the beautiful thing is that you are hiding God's truths in your heart that will lead to a happy life. If you can already read the stories yourself, tell Mom or Dad about it afterwards and see if they can find the treasure. What fun if they get it wrong!

Now off you go and enjoy yourself!

CONTENTS

MOTHER HEN

Josh and Jodi were up very early – today they were going to the farm for the entire weekend. Farmer Jake's farm! In no time at all they were up, dressed, breakfast done and standing at the front door waiting to be picked up. Their adventure was about to begin.

What an adventure it turned out to be. The next morning, Josh and Jodi woke up with the sound of a rooster crowing, "Cock-a-doodle-dooooo!"

The rooster urged them to get up! Get up quick! There were billows of smoke rising over the maize fields. They could see that Farmer Jake was very, very worried. He asked the children to stay indoors while he and his helpers tried to put out the blazing fire. A few hours later, he returned, dragging his feet. His shoulders drooped. His spirits were low. The fire had destroyed almost all of his crops.

The next day, Farmer Jake put on his gumboots and said, "Come, kids, let's go check out the damage." They were excited to get out of the house, but didn't expect what they were about to see! Oh dear! The fields were black. The ash was smoldering. Little traces of smoke were still rising from the ashes. Everything, but everything was black like charcoal. It was a sad sight.

And wherever Farmer Jake walked and whatever he kicked flew up as charcoal dust. He was really sad, and the children felt very sorry for him.

Suddenly, Farmer Jake kicked something that turned out to be more than just a tuft of burnt grass. The ashes rose up and three fluffy little chicks scurried out. It was the most amazing sight. But no one said a word. Farmer Jake just stood there, tears streaming down his cheeks. He sat the children down on a rock, one on either side of him and took their hands in his big, rough, dirty hands. The tears still racing down his cheeks and making pathways down his dirty face.

"I remember sitting in Sunday School, years ago," he began, "and hearing a similar story. The story was about Jesus who loved us so much that He died on a cross for us, so that we might be saved. And that is exactly what this mother hen has done. She loved her chicks so much that when she saw the danger coming, she gathered them under her wings and kept them safe. Safe and

cuddly and warm. She died in the fire, but they were saved. Just look at them running around free because of her sacrifice."

Farmer Jake reminded Josh and Jodi of John 3:16 that says: "For God so loved the world that He gave His one and only Son, that whoever believes in Him shall not perish but have eternal life."

Can you guess what our first treasure is?
JESUS LOVES ME

SOMETHING TO THANK GOD FOR

Thank You, Jesus, for loving me and all my family and friends. And thank You so much for dying for me and taking away my sins. You are just like a mother hen who gathers us safe under Your wings.
Amen.

SOMETHING TO DO

Cut out 3 yellow fluffy chicks from a magazine and paste them on a blank page. Now draw black dust and ashes all around them. Remember that they were safe under their mommy's wings.

JUST A PIECE OF PAPER

The sun was shining and Josh and Jodi were playing on the swings in the garden. Suddenly Jodi called out at the top of her voice, "Josh, does God love me?"

"Of course He does!" answered Josh.

Grammy, who had been dozing in her deckchair and heard the children talking, got up to fetch her Bible. She called the children over and they both huddled around her as she read John 3:16 to them. It was the same verse Farmer Jake shared with them on the farm:

> "For God so loved the world (that includes all of us) that He gave His one and only Son, that whoever believes in Him shall not perish but have eternal life."

"Jodi, I'm going to put your name in place of 'whoever' and see if it says something special to you," said Grammy. "For God so loved Jodi that He gave His one and only Son, that if Jodi believes in Him, Jodi shall not perish but Jodi shall have eternal life."

"Wow, Grammy, that's real cool. So God does love me after all. I must be so special to Him and I didn't even know it."

"Yes, and let me tell you about someone else who was special to Jesus. Have you ever heard of Martin Luther? He was a priest in Germany. But oh dear, he felt that he had to punish himself for all his sins. Sad, isn't it? But then one day as he was busy reading his Bible, he discovered that Jesus had died on a cross in his place and paid for his sins just because Jesus loved him. Those words hit Martin Luther hard. Right there and then, he thanked Jesus and accepted Him as his personal Savior. His life changed overnight! And all he wanted to do was to tell everybody else about the love of Jesus.

"Some time later, Martin Luther was having his Bible printed in Germany. The printer's daughter was happily humming a tune, walking around and picking up scraps of paper.

"As she gathered up the bits of fallen paper from the printing machine, a certain piece of paper caught her eye. On that piece of paper she read the words: 'For God so loved the world that He gave ...' That was it. The other piece was missing. But those words spoke to her heart, and suddenly she became aware of God's love. No one had ever told her about Jesus. And she didn't really feel

anything for God – besides fear. But when she read those words, 'For God so loved the world that He gave ...' her fear changed to joy.

"That evening her mother noticed the change in her daughter and asked her what had happened to her? Her daughter handed her the piece of paper from her pocket with the words: 'For God so loved the world that He gave ...' Her mother read it and asked, 'But what did God give, Darling?' Her daughter, quiet for a moment, answered sweetly, 'Mom, I don't know. But if He loved us so much to give us anything, we should not be afraid of Him. We should just love Him in return.'"

You can keep this treasure.

I AM SPECIAL!

SOMETHING TO THANK GOD FOR

Thank You, Jesus, that I am special to my mom and dad. But I am more special to You and that makes me feel extra loved. I love You soooo much! Amen.

SOMETHING TO DO

Write down on a piece of paper in one color: "For God so loved the world that He gave ..." And then write the rest of the Scripture verse in another color. Imagine how you would have felt if you had picked up that piece of paper.

A SPECIAL CARPENTER

Grandpa's hobby was woodwork. Often the smell of freshly oiled wood pulled the children magically inside his quaint little workshop. They loved to potter around. Picking up the odd nails. Kicking off their shoes. Feeling the sawdust between their toes.

One day, as Josh and Jodi came running out of grandpa's workshop, Grammy was reminded of a story. The children huddled around her to listen.

"This is a true story that took place long ago in America. There was a small church, the Loretto Chapel, also called the 'Chapel of Wonder'. This small church took five years to build. It had an altar, a pretty rose-colored window and a balcony with a choir loft where the choir sat. This choir loft is the reason for this story.

"In 1878 the nuns looked at this little chapel and felt sad. Everything was in place and finished. There were doors, pews and the floor had been laid. Even the choir loft was in place. But, there were no stairs to the loft. The little chapel was too small to have a normal staircase. So how would the choir members ever be able to get up to the loft? The best builders and designers just shook their heads and said, 'Impossible. We can't do it!' So the nuns of the Loretto Chapel decided that the only thing they could do was pray. And pray they did, for nine whole days.

"On the last day of their prayer time a bearded, sun-tanned Mexican carpenter arrived. With him he had a dreamy donkey carrying his

tools. He told them that he had heard they needed a staircase to a choir loft. And he thought that he might be able to help. So Mother Superior gave him permission to do the job. For at least six months he worked on the task with simple tools. No one was allowed inside the Chapel until he had completed his work. And then one glorious morning, as the nuns entered the Chapel, they found their prayers had been answered. There was their staircase, spiraling from the floor to the choir loft. It looked like a corkscrew! Beautiful!

"When the nuns turned around to thank the sun-tanned carpenter, he was gone! He was never seen again. He never asked for money or for praise. He was just a simple carpenter. He did what no one else could do. He made it possible for the singers to walk up the stairs to

the choir loft and sing their hearts out. No wonder they call it the 'Chapel of Wonder'.

"What an amazing answer to prayer. Who was this master carpenter? No one knows. The nuns believe he was sent by God. Maybe he was an angel!"

What treasure does this story make you think of?
GOD IS A GOD OF MIRACLES

SOMETHING TO DO

Paint or color a blank page with dark blue. Then paste stars all over and make your own moon. Imagine how excited God was when He created the heavens with the stars and the moon. Isn't He just great? Draw or paste a picture of an angel somewhere on your page to remind you that God is a God of miracles.

SOMETHING TO THANK GOD FOR

Thank You, Jesus, that You are still doing miracles today for us to see. You are such a good God. And You are a mighty, wonderful God! Amen.

WHEN THE TRUMPET SOUNDS

One Sunday evening Josh was sitting next to his mom in church, eating his favorite candy. Suddenly the pastor mentioned a trumpet, and Josh was all ears because he loved music. The pastor said that one day, in the twinkling of an eye, the trumpet will sound and all those who have put their faith and trust in Jesus, will rise up and meet Him in the air. Josh was worried, "What if I get left behind?"

When he got home he couldn't sleep. He kept thinking, "One day everyone will be caught up to meet Jesus in the air, and I'll be left behind, all on my own."

Josh quietly sneaked into his mother's bedroom, climbed on the bed and cuddled up close beside her. With her arm tightly wrapped around him, Josh told her everything. His mother just listened, and then she showed Josh how he could put his faith and trust in Jesus.

That night, Josh invited Jesus into his heart. Now he was sure that one day he will also be caught up in the air with all the others to meet Jesus. Josh couldn't wait to tell Jodi the good news.

The next morning there was a rush to have breakfast and be on time for school. Mom dropped them off at school, and as they all piled out of the car Josh grabbed Jodi's arm. He told her to meet him at the tuck shop at break time.

Finally, break time came and Josh told Jodi his news. He added, "Mom also told me that no one knows the date or the hour when Jesus will return. Not even the angels. Not even God's Son, Jesus ... only God the Father knows. We just have to watch and be ready."

Jodi had never really felt that it was necessary to invite Jesus into her heart because she thought she was a good girl. She didn't think that the wrong things she had done were sins. They were just mistakes. But Josh reminded her that even good people need Jesus.

"Jodi, remember what Mom said," Josh went on, "sometimes the mistakes we make are actually sins – because sin is doing what is wrong in God's eyes! Wanting your own way, doing, saying or thinking bad things – those are all sins. And not believing in Jesus is the biggest sin of all."

This is a very precious treasure.
JESUS WANTS ME TO BELONG TO HIM

SOMETHING TO THANK GOD FOR

Thank You, Jesus, that You gave Your life to save me from my sins, because You love me so much. I must go out and tell my friends about You so that they will also hear the trumpet and get caught up to meet You in the sky one day. Amen.

SOMETHING TO DO

Make a poster to put on your wall by drawing a beautiful, shiny trumpet. When your picture is completed, draw a cloud around it. Color it in, and at the bottom of your page write: JESUS IS COMING AGAIN!

CLIMBING TREES

Grammy enjoys telling Josh and Jodi stories from the Bible. Today she is reminded of the story of Zacchaeus as she watches Josh and Jodi climb a tree outside.

Zacchaeus was a very short man, who lived in a town called Jericho. He was a tax collector for the government, but he took more money from the people than he was supposed to. You see, he thought by keeping all that extra money he would become rich. The people didn't like him, because they knew what he was doing. He was stealing.

One day Zacchaeus heard that Jesus was coming to their town. But how could he see Jesus through the crowd if he was so short? So he thought and thought and came up with a clever plan. He would climb a sycamore tree and have the best view ever. After looking around, he found the perfect tree, right next to the road. No one would see him, but he could peep through the leaves.

And so began the climb, holding on tightly all the way right up to the top of the tree. Eventually he found the right branch to sit on and waited and waited. Then Jesus came. The next moment He was standing right below Zacchaeus. Jesus stopped. Maybe He was going to heal someone. But no, He looked up! *He's going to see me*, Zacchaeus thought! *What now?* "Zacchaeus," Jesus said, "Come down from that tree, because I'm coming to your house today."

Wow, He wants to visit with me in my house! No one had ever done that before. Zacchaeus was so excited that this time he nearly fell out of the tree, trying to scramble down in time to meet Jesus.

Jesus knew all about Zacchaeus, just like He knows all about you and me. He knew Zacchaeus had stolen money. And even though He didn't like what Zacchaeus had done, He loved him anyway.

As they entered his house, Zacchaeus suddenly felt so ashamed. "Jesus, I have been such a bad person. But I want to be different." There must have been tears streaming down his face as he said those words. "No one likes me. I have stolen money from the people. And I'm so ashamed to tell You this. But I want to give each person *four* times as much as what I have stolen from them! Please forgive me, Jesus, and help me to be a better person," Zacchaeus pleaded.

Jesus was touched. Even though He didn't like what he had done, He loved this man. He saw his heart. He put His arms around him and said, "Son, I forgive you! Now go in peace."

After Grammy had finished telling Josh and Jodi the story of Zacchaeus, she asked: "What do you think the people did when Zacchaeus paid them back? I think they must have thought that he was crazy! But there must have been so much rejoicing with a big, big party! And who do you think paid for it all? Zacchaeus of course!

"What about you? Has someone hurt you lately? Or, spread ugly rumors about you and because of that you have lost a friend? Forgive them. Don't hold a grudge. Be nice to them. Treat them as if they've never hurt you!

"Do you remember Jesus' prayer on the cross? He prayed: 'Father, forgive them, for they do not know what they are doing' (Luke 23:34). What a beautiful example for us to follow!"

This treasure will
surprise you!
JESUS FORGIVES

SOMETHING TO DO

Write a short letter to someone and ask them to forgive you for something you said or did that hurt them.

SOMETHING TO THANK GOD FOR

Dear Lord Jesus, thank You for forgiving Zacchaeus. Please help me to be nice to others. I want to be a happy person so that my friends will have fun spending time with me.
Amen.

STOLEN GOODS

Grammy went to pick Josh and Jodi up from their music lesson. As they drove off, Jodi asked, "Does God see everything we do, Grammy?" and Grammy assured her that He does.

"Well," said Jodi, "I'm so embarrassed about it. I took some money from Dad's wallet on his desk. You see, I needed money for the tuck shop. After I did it, I felt terrible. But it was too late. Because I had done something so very wrong, I was afraid. Afraid that I would be caught out! Afraid that I might be punished. I couldn't even run to meet Dad when he came home from work, because I felt so guilty. I couldn't look him in the eye.

"Finally I could stand it no longer. I ran to Dad and threw my arms around his neck. I cried and cried and told him everything. I told him how sorry I was and that I would never do it again. He just listened. He didn't even scold me. Instead, we talked a lot about stealing. He read Exodus 20:15 to me: 'You must not steal.' It was then that I realized stealing is not a mistake, it's a sin! Dad put his arms around me and forgave me. He even thanked me for telling the truth. I felt so loved, in spite of what I had done.

"I also thanked Jesus for His forgiveness. Of course I had to return the money, but that was fine by me."

"I'm glad you told your dad," Grammy added, "because when we tell lies, we are really hurting ourselves. Because we have to live with that lie. And sometimes it leads to another lie and then another and another and so it goes on. Some children think that as long as they don't get caught out, it's okay. But it will keep bugging them. They are actually sinning against God. It makes Him sad."

Then she told Josh and Jodi the story about Achan in the Bible: "Do you remember how the people of Israel marched around Jericho seven times? After the priests had blown their trumpets and the people shouted, the walls of Jericho came tumbling down. The Lord told Joshua to tell the people to destroy everything and everybody, because Jericho was very wicked. The people of Israel were to take nothing for themselves.

"But, a man named Achan thought that if he just took a garment, a big piece of gold and two hundred shekels of silver no one would

ever know about it. So he did just that and made his way to his tent. He dug a hole in the ground of his tent and buried his stolen goods in the ground. Now he was rich!

"The next city the Israelites had to conquer was a city called Ai. But the army of Ai defeated the Israelites. When Joshua heard that they had been defeated, he fell to the ground and prayed to God. God knew what Achan had done. And that's why God allowed Israel to be defeated. God told Joshua that Achan was the man who disobeyed Him. So Achan was brought before Joshua. Can you imagine how he must have felt? And when Achan was confronted, he owned up. But he had to carry the consequences of his deeds, and he was punished. They took Achan to a valley nearby, together with his family, all his flocks and herds and all the things that he had stolen. They then stoned him. A very sad ending for a dishonest man."

You must value this treasure:
GOD WANTS US TO ALWAYS OWN UP

SOMETHING TO THANK GOD FOR

Dear Lord Jesus, I'm so sorry that at times I make You sad. When You are sad, I am sad. But thank You that You forgive me and still love me. Amen.

SOMETHING TO DO

Draw and make up your own bank note. Write on it: Honesty is the best policy!

A DAY FILLED WITH HEARTS

It was Valentine's Day! Josh and Jodi came marching through the front door, waving their Valentine's cards in the air.

"Look how many cards we got!" they shrieked. "And even one from Johnny!" Grammy interrupted them and said, "Let me tell you how special Johnny is. I bumped into his mom at the store this afternoon. She told me that he was not a very popular boy, but the night before Valentine's Day he had worked till late making a card for everyone in his class. Sad to say he never received one himself. But after school, when his mother met him at the bus stop, he was radiant: "Mom, I didn't forget anyone!"

Grammy loved to see her grandchildren so happy. "Valentine's Day is a day filled with lots of hearts!" she said. "I want to share two different kinds of hearts with you. Our first heart is when you put your hand over your heart and feel it beating. The doctors have a special instrument called a stethoscope that allows them to listen to your heartbeat.

"The second heart is the heart we speak of when we invite Jesus to enter into our lives. That's the real you. The real you is the soul that lives in your body. So when you invite Jesus to come into your heart, He comes to live in your life, through His Spirit, not by His body, for He took His body to heaven with Him."

Suddenly, Grammy burst out laughing. "This reminds me of the story of one little boy called Duane. He was enjoying his favorite

meal, Macaroni and Cheese, right after he had accepted Jesus into his heart. He surprised the family by telling them that he knew what Jesus was having for supper. Of course everyone wanted to know what it was!

"'Macaroni and Cheese,' he blurted out, 'because now that Jesus is in my heart, He must also be eating what I am eating.'"Thankfully his dad was able to explain to him that when Jesus went back to heaven after His death, burial and resurrection, He took His earthly body with Him. So now, when He comes into our hearts, He comes in with His Spirit, not His body."

"Yes," said Jodi, "The other evening, after Dad read a Bible story, he asked us whether we were sure that Jesus lived in our hearts. I really wanted to be sure that He did. So Dad read Revelation 3:20 to us: 'Here I am! I stand at the door and knock. If anyone hears My voice and opens the door, I will come in.'

"Dad explained that Jesus had been knocking at my heart's door for a long time and at last I heard Him knocking. I was so ready and then I prayed this prayer: 'Dear Lord Jesus, I believe that You died on the cross for me. You took the punishment for my sins. I am sorry for doing wrong and sinful things. Please come into my heart and forgive all my sins. I accept You as my own personal Savior. Amen.'"

Share this treasure with others:
JESUS WANTS TO LIVE IN MY HEART

SOMETHING TO THANK GOD FOR

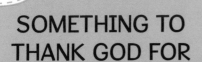

Thank You, Jesus, that if I ask You to come into my heart, You will do it and You will change me. I will become a better person. Amen.

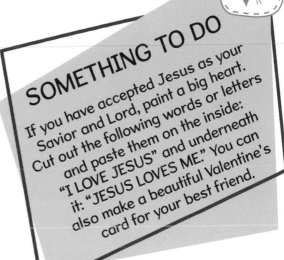

SOMETHING TO DO

If you have accepted Jesus as your Savior and Lord, paint a big heart. Cut out the following words or letters and paste them on the inside: "I LOVE JESUS" and underneath it: "JESUS LOVES ME." You can also make a beautiful Valentine's card for your best friend.

A VISITOR CAME KNOCKING

Josh and Jodi were helping their dad clean the pool. It was a beautiful day. Maybe a little bit windy because the leaves kept falling into the pool. But this was a job Josh and Jodi really loved to do, because it was fun time spent with Dad. No interruptions. No laptop. No cell phone. Just talking and sharing and laughing. But this particular Saturday, something was troubling Jodi.

"Dad, what if you invite Jesus to come into your heart and you do something terribly wrong. Will He go out of your heart?" Jodi asked.

"Jodi, I'm going to answer your question with a question," said Dad. "Suppose you come to see me, and you knock at my door. I open and say, 'Come in,' and you come in and sat down. Then I shut the door and we start talking. What would you think of me if I kept saying to you, 'Jodi, please come in. Please come in'?

"You would probably think that I had lost my mind, and tell me, 'Dad, can't you see that I am already inside? Why do you keep asking me to come in?' In the same way, what do you suppose the Lord Jesus thinks when you keep on asking Him to come into your heart when He is already there? He tells us in Hebrews 13:5 that when He enters our lives, He comes in to stay. He will never leave us. Never ever! And Jodi, we can trust Him. If you've done a bad thing, it makes Him sad. But when you ask Him to forgive you, He will do it. He will never leave you because He loves you."

Jodi quickly fetched her Bible and together they read Hebrews 13:5: "I will never leave you."

"Now let's use the fingers on our right hand as we say it together. Begin with the little finger and pointing to yourself with the thumb on the word "you". I – WILL – NEVER – LEAVE – YOU. That is very special, isn't it? This will remind you forever that He will always be in your heart, no matter what! So, when you do something wrong, do you need to ask Jesus to come into your heart again?"

"No," said Jodi confidently, "because He is already there. I just need to tell Jesus how sorry I am and ask Him to forgive me, and He will."

This treasure will help you
when you're feeling lonely:
GOD WILL NEVER LEAVE ME

SOMETHING TO THANK GOD FOR

Dear Lord Jesus, it is so precious
to know that I can always feel
safe because You said that
You will never leave me.
Thank You!
Amen.

SOMETHING TO DO

Take an old photo frame
and decorate with feathers.
Place a photo of yourself in
the frame and write this verse
below the photo: "He will
cover you with His feathers,
and under His wings you will
find refuge." (Psalm 91:4)

A FRIEND IN NEED

Levi and Rachi were two fun-loving children who happened to be twins. One of their classmates Matthew had just been diagnosed with sarcoma, which is bone cancer, and was very weak and not able to attend school. Levi and Rachi were devastated. They loved Matthew. He was so much fun to be with and he was very good at all ball games. So they asked their mom to take them to Matthew's house.

Arriving at the front door they knocked, not knowing what to expect. But oh dear! It was a tiny little home and it wasn't a happy visit because Matthew was pale and sad and tired. Too tired to even play ball with them. His lunch consisted only of a peach and some tea. They wondered how he could get strong with so little food.

That night, as they were gazing out the window, thinking about what they could do for Matthew … they suddenly spotted movement … Someone was actually stealing peaches from their trees in the back garden. "Let's go and catch him," they whispered. So they grabbed a flashlight and quietly crept behind a bush. Switching on their flashlight they got a big fright … "Oh no!" said a disappointed Levi. "We were about to catch the thief." Instead it was their mom picking peaches. She immediately jumped with surprise. She told them that she was picking peaches for Matthew. It was his favorite fruit. She wanted to pick them now so that she could deliver them tomorrow when she went to visit Matthew's mom. They quickly helped her pick some more peaches.

The next weekend they had to spend with their dad. And the first thing they did was to beg him to find some branches and sticks and ropes. "Whatever for, Kids?" he asked. So they told him the whole story about Matthew. They wanted to build him his very own tepee, as a little hide-out. So no problem to Dad, he managed to get everything they needed in no time at all. What's more, he even suggested they go and build it that very weekend, so Matthew could be there to see it all happen. Excitedly they phoned and Matthew's mom was ecstatic! "Come now! Come straight away! He would just love it!"

When they arrived at Matthew's house they got busy straight away, passing branches and sticks as Dad needed them, giggling and laughing all the way. It took them the whole morning. But what fun! Eventually it was finally completed. They stepped aside to look at their brilliant creation. It was just perfect! Matthew couldn't

wait and crawled inside to try it out. The next moment he was at the entrance, peeping out at them, beaming from ear to ear. "Thank you! Thank you! Thank you!" he shouted out.

The next visit was different because Matthew had an appointment to see the doctor. His mom asked if they would like to go with Matthew, as he really looked forward to their visits. They were delighted! But of course it meant waiting and waiting and waiting in the doctor's room!

Eventually Matthew and his mom came out but she was crying. Levi and Rachi's mom went up to her and just held her tight. In between her sobbing, Matthew's mom blurted out that the treatment needed for his illness was going to cost her the earth. And she just didn't have the money. On hearing that, something started ticking in Levi's mind on their way home.

Can you spot this treasure?
I WILL BE KIND TO OTHERS

SOMETHING TO THANK GOD FOR

Dear Lord Jesus, thank You for family and friends. Please help me to be nice to them. Where I can help or do something to make them smile, please help me to do just that. Amen.

SOMETHING TO DO

Think of something you can do to help someone, like washing the dishes, carrying someone's books, etc. Now go out and do it.

A FRIEND IN NEED (CONTINUED)

When they got home Levi made a bee line for his piggy bank and asked Rachi to bring hers too. They emptied out the contents of both their savings on the floor and started counting.

And so on their next visit, there stood Matthew's mom in the kitchen. Levi, who was always up to tricks, asked her to hold the ends of her apron out in front of her. Not knowing what was coming next, she did just that. And into the apron the children threw their money.

"What is this?" she gasped when she saw the money. They excitedly told her that it was all their savings for Matthew's treatment. She was speechless. Again tears started trickling down her cheeks. "This is wonderful. Thank you so much, but I think you should give this money to the doctor yourself."

The next day they were excitedly sitting in the doctor's waiting room. The kind doctor walked towards them wondering what their problem could be. They told him that they had collected some money and asked him if it would be enough to cover Matthew's treatment. "You see, sir, his mom is very poor and she just doesn't have the money." The doctor took the money from them, poured it onto the counter and counted it out loud. He stopped short to mop a tear from his eye: "Wow! It's the perfect amount!" he said. "That's exactly what the treatment will cost. May I keep it? I will

contact Matthew's mom in the morning." The twins left the rooms beaming, feeling on top of the world.

What they didn't know was that there was a wealthy, wealthy man who was next in line with his little daughter beside him. And on hearing their story, tears were running down his cheeks. "I know it's not enough," he said to the doctor, "but I would like to make up the shortfall for that little boy's treatment." The doctor again stopped short to mop a tear from the other eye. This was all too much for him. But he agreed to go ahead with the treatment.

For the next few months Levi and Rachi visited Matthew often. Even though he was often in pain, they watched him getting stronger and stronger until eventually he was back at school again and even playing ball games.

One evening the children had been invited for supper to Matthew's house, and that particular evening Matthew went to bed early as he had had an exhausting day. They stood around his bed and shared with him many delightful stories. They also shared the story of The Good Shepherd, who cared for His sheep and gave

His life for His sheep. Of course they were talking about the Lord Jesus. Matthew listened. He loved the story. He wanted to hear it over and over again. They told him about the Good News of Jesus coming to die for our sins and giving eternal life to anyone who asked Him to come into their hearts. Matthew stopped them right there and then said: "I want to belong to that Shepherd." So right there and then Matthew prayed to accept Jesus into his heart. They all knew that Jesus would take care of Matthew and help him through his illness.

And with that peaceful expression on his face, the twins left him, quietly tip-toeing out of his bedroom. They were so grateful that they were able to help him through his difficult time. But how special that the Good Shepherd had found his lost sheep – Matthew!

You can't keep this treasure to yourself.
I WILL TELL OTHERS ABOUT JESUS

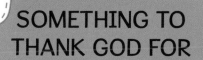

SOMETHING TO THANK GOD FOR

Dear Lord Jesus, thank You for being my Shepherd. Help me to tell others how much You care for us. Amen.

SOMETHING TO DO

Using a blanket and some chairs, build a tepee for you and your friends to play in.

WINNING THE BATTLE

Josh was fascinated by watching his little brother Naethan and a friend playing Lego. They built a huge castle with a draw bridge, turrets and everything else that goes with it. They were totally carried away by their game – armed knights, guns, bows and arrows, pirates getting out of their boats ready to attack. After they had been playing for a while, Josh spoke to them.

"Guys, listen to this story that I heard at Sunday school. It's a true story from the Bible. Our teacher reminded us that the best book to read is the Bible. And when you listen to this story you will see that God is the God of the impossible ...

"The Philistines were a wicked nation and the Israelites were God's nation. So, when the Philistines heard that David had been crowned king of Israel, they tried to capture him, but David found out about their plan. He went straight to the Lord and asked Him, 'Shall I go and fight against these Philistines or will You defeat them for me?' God said, 'Yes! Go and fight against these Philistines and I will give you victory over them.'

"So David went out and fought them at a place called Baal-Perazim and defeated them. 'The Lord did it!' cried David with so much excitement. 'We won!' But the Philistines weren't going to give up that easily. They came back to fight some more. Again David asked God for advice. This time, God gave him a very interesting command: 'Don't attack them from the front. Go behind them and come out from behind the mulberry trees. When you hear a

sound like marching feet coming from the tops of the mulberry trees, then you must attack! It will be a sign that the Lord has prepared the way for you and you will destroy them.' You see God was going to work in a supernatural way, in a way only God can. The Lord did it again. The Philistines were destroyed. And this time they did not come back.'

"Our God is so big, so strong and so mighty, there's nothing our God cannot do!

"You mean even when someone is about to fight with me at school, God can help me?" asked Naethan.

"Yes!" answered Josh, "Just quietly ask God to help you control yourself, there and then and He will. But of course you need to be kind to that boy first and then God will help him change his attitude towards you. Remember God is the God of the impossible."

What treasure does Nathan uncover here?
GOD WILL ALWAYS HELP ME

SOMETHING TO THANK GOD FOR

Dear Lord Jesus, thank You that I can ask You to help me with anything, and You will. Even when I don't like someone, You will help me to love them.
Amen.

SOMETHING TO DO

Try to draw the Bible story, or a scene from it, on a piece of paper. Tell the story to your family during family Bible study.

A SING-ALONG SONG

One day Grammy asked Jodi and Josh, "Did you know that God can use anybody in His big plan, even a little child like you? There is a beautiful story in the Bible about a little girl who was used by God.

"She was just a little slave girl. A little girl who lost her mommy and daddy, and who was now working in the home of a general, called Naaman. Now a general is the head of an army. She could have been bitter because Naaman's soldiers had killed her family, but she wasn't. She was worried about him. He was very sick. He had a skin disease called leprosy, and no one was allowed to go near him.

"Naaman desperately needed help and he didn't know where to find it. Little did he realize that the little slave girl had the answer. She went to her mistress and told her about Elisha, a prophet in the land of Israel, where she came from. 'Elisha can heal him,' she told her mistress.

"So Naaman went off to see Elisha so that he could heal him. But Elisha didn't even bother to come out of his house and meet him. Instead he sent his servant. *That's strange*, thought Naaman, *doesn't he know who I am. I am Naaman, the General!* Ouch! He was a proud man. And what's more, the servant told him to wash himself seven times in a dirty river. *No ways*, he thought. But then he changed his mind, and did as he was told. *Voila!* He looked and looked again. His skin was smooth. It was perfect! Yes, everything was as it used to be. He could even hug his wife again. Then Elisha came out and refused any money. 'God has healed you!' he said. And you know what else happened? God healed Naaman's heart of all the ugly pride. All of this happened because a little slave girl had a caring heart.

"And do you know what? God still uses little children today, sometimes even without them knowing about it!

"I have a friend who at one time was feeling very down. Her husband had passed away, and on top of it she had the flu. When she walked into the pharmacy to buy medicine, two little girls were sitting on the chairs in the waiting area. They were between four and six years-old. She found out later that their names were Jaz and Roxy. Jaz and Roxy were dressed like princesses and were singing while they waited for their mommy. Their song was all about being strong and of good courage and not to be afraid because God is with us wherever we go.

"What they didn't realize was that my friend was listening closely to the words of their song. When their mom came to fetch them,

my friend told her that she had lost her husband and felt very sad and depressed. It was the hardest thing for her to return to church. But the little girls' singing got her thinking. The girls' mom sympathized with my friend and then suggested that she go back to church where she would be loved and helped. With a big 'thank you!' and a sparkle in her eye, my friend gave lollipops to both Jaz and Roxy, and then she left.

"She told me later that she went back to church the very next Sunday, and that she joined a care group with other women who lost their husbands too. Isn't it amazing how God can use even very young children like you?"

Do you need a clue for this treasure?
GOD CAN USE EVEN ME!

SOMETHING TO DO

Make a nice card for someone who is sick or feeling a bit down. Ask your mom or dad to help you take it to them.

SOMETHING TO THANK GOD FOR

Dear Lord Jesus,
thank You for using
little kids in Your great,
big and wonderful plan for
us. Please use me too.
I am ready any day
and any time.
Amen.

A PRISON DRAMA

This is Grammy's favorite story: "King Herod was a wicked king. He didn't like Peter telling others about Jesus. So, he put him in prison with sixteen soldiers to guard him. There was no chance of escape. He wanted Peter to be put to death after the Passover, but Peter's friends were praying for him.

"The night before Peter was to die he was fast asleep in his cell chained between two soldiers. Suddenly there was a bright light in his cell. An angel stood right beside Peter! He slapped Peter on his side and woke him.

"'Quick! Get up!' the angel said. Peter rubbed his eyes, he wasn't sure if he was dreaming. But he did as he was told and the chains around his wrists fell off. *Could he be dreaming*, he wondered. No! The angel then told him to put on his shoes and coat, and to follow him. He did that and they left the cell together, arriving at the big iron gates leading onto the street. Wow, the gates just opened up by themselves and they walked right through. He was free! No one was following them!

"After they walked a bit further, the angel left him. *What should I do now*, Peter wondered. He was confused. *The Lord must have sent His angel to save me*, he thought. He realized then that his friends weren't going to believe what they saw. So he ran as fast as he could go to tell them.

"His friends were busy praying for him. He knocked on the door. When the servant girl opened the door, she was stunned! She just

closed the door in his face and left him standing there. She ran back inside to tell the others, but they wouldn't believe her. Peter just kept on knocking and knocking and knocking. Eventually they opened the door slowly and peeped out. And there he stood.

"'Peter!' they screamed. 'It's you after all! It's *really you!*' They pushed open the door, pulled him inside and even pinched him to make sure it was really him.

"'Our prayers have been answered!' they shouted, and danced around praising God, just like you and I would have done. Can you imagine the excitement for the rest of the evening?

Because Peter listened to the angel he was set free from jail. What if he had not listened to the angel? He would have made the wrong choice.

Peter put this treasure into action:
GOD HELPS ME TO MAKE GOOD CHOICES

SOMETHING TO THANK GOD FOR

Dear Lord Jesus, thank You for helping Peter. I need You to help me listen carefully and make good choices just like Peter. Please help me every day. I need Your help because I can't do it on my own. You have all the wisdom in the world. Amen.

SOMETHING TO DO

Paste a picture of someone on your journal page. Then cut out long strips of black paper and paste it over the picture leaving gaps between the black strips, so that it looks like prison bars. In the right-hand corner at the top of your page, paste a picture or a sticker of an angel. Underneath you can write: God is a God of miracles!

THE WELL-DESERVED MEDAL

"You all know that it is wrong to lie about things," Grammy said. "You should also not do things that you know are wrong. This is known as being honest, and God expects all of His children to be honest. The story of Kyra is a good example of what honesty looks like.

"Kyra always longed to win a medal at a sports event. As you know, to win a medal for a race, you have to come first to get gold, second to get silver and third to get a bronze medal.

"On this particular sports day, Kyra did her very best in her first race, but only came in sixth place. The teacher, however, made a big mistake and placed her third. Before she knew what was happening, she was on the podium receiving her bronze medal. Her mom, sitting on the grandstand, knew it wasn't right and prayed that the Lord would show her what to do. Well, Kyra came running to her mom very excitedly with the bronze medal around her neck and said, 'Look what I've got, Mom! Do you know what Mom, I didn't come third. I actually came sixth.' And her mom agreed.

"So her mom asked her if she knew which girl had come third. Kyra did and knew exactly where the other girl was sitting. Her mom then suggested that maybe she should give the medal to the girl. It was a very difficult thing to ask of Kyra, and she held tightly onto the medal. She knew that it would be dishonest to keep it, because she didn't really deserve it. And you can't enjoy what you didn't deserve. Then her dad who was right there listening to it all, realized he should step in and suggested he go with her. After thinking about it, Kyra decided that it was the right thing to do. When they reached the other girl, Kyra handed her the bronze medal that was rightly hers. Both the mom and the other girl were delighted.

"Then God took over again and did something very exciting for Kyra. Her team ran the relay race and they came first! So she got her medal after all, and this time it was a gold one. This made Kyra realize that it is better to get a medal the right way than it is to get a medal that you never really deserved. The teachers however heard what Kyra had done and at the end of the day, when all the events were over, Kyra was called up to the podium and presented with a bronze medal for HONEST SPORTMANSHIP. Imagine her joy on her way home.

"God taught Kyra all about being honest and gave her something amazing because she did the right thing. It is always better to be honest! Imagine what a happy girl she was when she finally arrived home."

Kyra earned this treasure:
JESUS IS PLEASED WHEN I TELL THE TRUTH

SOMETHING TO THANK GOD FOR

Dear Lord Jesus, thank You for reminding me that honesty is the best policy. I want my friends and family to be able to trust me. It will make me feel like a better person. Amen.

SOMETHING TO DO

What medal would you like to receive one day? For example, a medal for honesty, helpfulness, kindness, sport or music. Now design your own medal on paper to put on your wall as a reminder of what you want to achieve.

THE BLACK MAMBA

"Today's story is about obedience. Yes, that thing we all find difficult to do sometimes," Grammy smiled. "God wants His children to obey their mommy and daddy. And don't you agree that life is so much easier and more fun when you listen to Mommy and Daddy? This reminds me of the story of Blaise and how his obedience saved his life.

"Blaise and his dad went for a long hike along the Nature Trail. They loved their time together, just the two of them. No one to bother them, they could enjoy the beautiful nature God had created. As Blaise was walking up ahead, he suddenly heard his dad frantically calling out to him: 'Blaise! Stop just where you are!' So he stopped. 'Duck!' So he did. 'Down on all fours!' Blaise wasn't sure what was going on, but he knew that he could trust his dad so he did everything exactly the way his dad told him to. 'Keep crawling! Crawl slowly to the left!' Obediently he did that too. 'Now get up and run as fast as you can!' And with that Blaise was up and running for all he was worth. Eventually he stopped, huffing and puffing, and waited for his dad to catch up with him.

"Blaise wondered what that was all about. When his dad reached him, Blaise realized that his dad had saved his life. Because you see, Blaise was walking under a tree, and so busy admiring nature that he didn't notice the black mamba hanging right above him. He didn't see it, but his dad did. His dad also knew that if he shouted, "Snake!" Blaise would get such a fright that he might do something

he shouldn't do. That's why he decided to get Blaise away from the snake before he told him anything. On the way back, his dad told him all about black mambas and he felt very glad that he had listened to his dad.

"Black mambas are one of Africa's most feared and respected snakes. And it is one of the fastest and deadliest snakes in the world. Just two drops of its venom can kill a person. If someone is bitten by a black mamba and they are far from a hospital, they need a helicopter to air-lift them to the nearest hospital, otherwise they will die. Can you believe that!

"Can you imagine how glad Blaise was that he had listened to his dad telling him what to do? Just imagine if he was disobedient and just carried on walking. He might have been bitten by the snake.

"Wow, what an important lesson he learned that day – listen and obey your parents!"

This treasure is a must:
GOD WANTS ME TO OBEY MY PARENTS

SOMETHING TO THANK GOD FOR

Dear Lord Jesus, thank You for my special, wonderful parents who always want the best for me. Help me to obey them straight away and not argue with them, talk back to them or sulk.
Amen.

SOMETHING TO DO

Draw a snake on a blank piece of paper. Then add scary-looking fangs. You can also take a thin piece of string, put glue on the one end and fold the tip backwards to make a head. Run glue on the one side of your string and glue it onto your page all wiggly just like a snake. Write on the snake: "I have to listen to Mom and Dad."

NINE UNGRATEFUL MEN

"Thank you, Grammy!" Josh and Jodi blurted out in unison. The children's good manners make Grammy feel so proud.

"Let me tell you a story from the Bible about ten men with leprosy, an awful skin disease, who were healed by Jesus. You might wonder where the doctors were and why no one helped them. You see, leprosy is such a terrible disease that you have to stay far away from lepers otherwise you can catch their disease. They had to go and live far outside of town. It was a very lonely life. And whenever the lepers saw someone coming along the road, they had to ring their little bells frantically. It was to remind people not to come close to them.

"Well, on this particular day, the sick men saw Jesus walking towards them. They asked Jesus to heal them. And so Jesus, the best doctor ever, healed them all and sent them on their way. But a very sad thing happened. Only one leper went back to thank Jesus. Jesus actually looked around and asked, 'Where are the other nine lepers?' Doesn't that tell you that Jesus wants us to be thankful for everything?"

"What are you thankful for, Grammy?" Josh asked.

"I am thankful for all of God's blessings," said Grammy, "and I'm also very thankful for certain people. Do you know the story of Uncle Michael? Well, one morning as I was reading Ephesians 4:29: "Don't use foul language. Let everything you say be good and helpful so that your words will be an encouragement to those who hear them," his name was written in the margin of my Bible. I had written it there a long time ago to remind me of the time when I walked into his bedroom and found him reading his Bible. This was the Scripture verse he read to me. I will never forget it. It reminds me to be kind to others and not to say ugly things to them. I am so grateful for the guidance we get when reading the Bible.

Then another precious little girl, Mia, obeyed this verse in the Bible when she complimented her brother. "I love your Superman cape. It makes you look real great!!" That comment made him feel real cool because she built him up. But if she had said to him: "That Superman cape sucks. You look plain stupid in it!" Imagine how he would have

felt then? Stupid! And she would have broken him down so badly. Our words hurt or make others happy. Why not thank Mom and Dad for all the things they do for you and see what it does for them!

Nine unhappy men
forgot to use this treasure:
I MUST REMEMBER TO
ALWAYS SAY "THANK YOU"

SOMETHING TO THANK GOD FOR

Think of something very special that happened to you this week and thank God in your own words. This will remind you to thank Jesus every day for what He does for you and for what He means to you.

SOMETHING TO DO

Write a letter of thanks to Jesus: "Dear Lord Jesus, thank You for ..."

GOD'S PHONE NUMBER

Ring, ring. Ring, ring.
"Hello?" ... "Hello Grammy, it's Leeza."
"Oh Leeza, I've missed you."

And that's what makes mobile phones so great. We can be so grateful that we have them today, because there was a time when there were no mobile phones. Now you can just pick up your phone, dial a number and talk to someone you love.

"Did you know that we can just as easily talk to Jesus?" Grammy asked Josh and Jodi after she had gotten off the phone with Leeza, their cousin. "That's what prayer is all about. Prayer is not only *talking* to Jesus, but also getting to *know* Him."

"In Jeremiah 33:3 we read: 'Call to Me and I will answer you.' Jesus doesn't really have a phone number, but just think of the number 333 for Jeremiah 33:3 when you want to talk to Him.

"It is a clever way to remember where in the Bible you can find this verse. God tells us in His word that we can call Him at any time and He *will* answer us. Isn't that great?

"Did you know that Jesus' 'phone' is never engaged? He is never too busy for you. He is always there to listen to you when you call. You can call Him at any time; early in the morning or before you go to school. Even in the middle of the day when you are having a hard

time with a friend. What about in the middle of the night when you're afraid?

"Do you remember the time Leeza asked for something special for her birthday? She told me, 'Grammy, please can I have an orange handbag. But please put pink glasses, blue earrings, a scarf and a hat inside. Not an umbrella, because it is not raining here.'

"I was so happy that I could give her everything on her wish list. As far as I'm able, I also like to give you everything you ask for. God is the same. He longs to give us what we ask Him. But because He is so wise, He doesn't always give us what we *want*. Sometimes He rather

gives us what we *need.* Do you know why? Because sometimes what we want isn't good for us.

"I remember when your little brother Naethan was 4 years old he wanted a three-speed bike for his birthday. His dad knew better and gave him a bike that was just right for him. You see if he had given Naethan what he wanted, he might have been sitting with bruises and cuts and maybe even a broken arm. Just like Naethan's dad knew what was best for him, so God knows what is best for us.

"God knows exactly what we need, even before we ask Him for it. But we must still talk to God, because He loves spending time with us and giving us the very best."

Use this treasure daily:
I CAN TALK TO JESUS EVERY DAY

SOMETHING TO THANK GOD FOR

Thank You, Jesus, that You are always there when I want to talk to You. And You are never too busy for me. I would like to talk to You every day and I know You look forward to hearing my voice too. Amen.

SOMETHING TO DO

Make a list of everything you've ever asked God for and mark what He has given you. Thank God for knowing what is best for you and for giving you everything you need.

THE MISSING TOY

Grammy was visiting Jesse when disaster struck! Jesse lost two of his Lego knights. It was the end of his little world and no one saw his tears. But Grammy did. So she helped him look. While she was on the ground searching she looked at him and said, "Jesse, when I can't find something, like my car keys, I ask Jesus to help me find them. I tell Jesus that I know He can see my keys. So He must please show me where they are. And He does."

So they prayed. They asked Jesus to show them where the knights were hiding. Then they looked and looked, and as they walked towards the fireplace, there they were! "Jesse, you see! Jesus has shown us where your two Lego knights were hiding!" Grammy exclaimed. But Jesse insisted that he found them himself. "No," Grammy reminded him, "we have just asked Jesus to show us, and He did. Isn't He great?"

A few days later Jesse's bouncing ball went missing. He remembered what Grammy had told him and he started looking and praying. Suddenly there, squashed under a cushion, was his bouncing ball. Jesse shouted with delight: "Isn't Jesus great? He showed me where to look!" He learned something about prayer and he thanked God.

A few weeks later his dad came back from his overseas trip. The whole family jumped in the car to go out for ice cream as a special treat. They were so excited. But suddenly Dad stopped the car. He remembered that in the rush, he had put his cell phone and wallet on the roof of the car. They all jumped out and started searching around.

Eventually Dad suggested that they form a circle and he asked little Jesse to pray. "Dear Jesus, please put love in the person's heart to bring back Daddy's wallet and phone. Amen."

Believe it or not, shortly afterwards, a man phoned. He told them that he had been walking around looking for a job when he found the wallet and phone lying in the road. He wanted to return it. The family met him at a certain place, got the phone and wallet back, and gave him a whopping reward. Dad then told a local newspaper what had happened. Shortly after the story was published, the man was offered a job! With a twinkle in his eye, Dad asked Jesse to thank Jesus. "Dear Lord Jesus, thank You for putting love in the man's

THE GOOD NEWS

NEWS THAT YOU ALWAYS WANT TO READ BECAUSE IT GIVES GOD THE GLORY

NEWS FLASH: Important people have discovered that eating vegetables makes you very smart. This discovery came after the important people ate some carrots and then answered difficult questions. They knew all the answers. Now everybody is buying carrots. Are you?

HERO RETURNS
WALLET & CELL PHONE

A passerby picked up a wallet and cell phone and returned it to the rightful owner.

Story by: JOY MOL

Jesse's dad left his cell phone and wallet on the roof of his car. A passerby who had been looking for a job, discovered the lost property lying in the road.

He met the family and returned the cell phone and wallet. This man's kindness and honesty will be rewarded.

See inside for full story …

heart to bring back Dad's wallet and phone. Please help Daddy never to put his phone and wallet on the roof again. Amen."

The prayer of a child is very precious to God. We can always listen for His sweet voice deep down inside of our hearts.

Wow! This treasure makes you feel important:
GOD HEARS AND ANSWERS PRAYER

SOMETHING TO DO

Think of all the different things that you have lost and found again! Remember to thank Jesus for helping you find them.

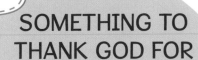

SOMETHING TO THANK GOD FOR

Thank You, dear Lord Jesus, that when I lose something I can always ask You to help me find it and You will. You can see everything. You are a great, big, wonderful God. Amen.

BROWN OR BLUE EYES

Amy Carmichael had beautiful brown eyes. But when she was little, she so badly wanted blue eyes like her mom. Her mom often told her that God hears and answers prayer. One night, folding her little hands, she got down on her knees beside her bed and asked God to give her blue eyes. She was so excited that night when she climbed into bed because in the morning she would have blue eyes, just like her mother. Why? Because she told herself: "God hears and answers prayer."

Well, early the next morning, she climbed onto a chair to look into the mirror. She wanted to burst into tears because she saw her eyes were still brown. God hadn't heard her prayer after all.

She went to her mom and blurted out that God hadn't answered her prayer. Her mother, however, very gently told her that sometimes when we ask God for something, He says, "No." Sometimes He says, "Wait!" And at other times He says, "Yes!" It reminds me of a traffic light. Red for "STOP!" Orange for "Wait!" and Green for "Go!"

God did answer her prayer that day, but His answer was no, because He knew what He wanted for her life even before she was born. So little Amy learned that "No" was also an answer. But there *is* a wonderful ending to her story. You see, God had a plan for her life, and her brown eyes were given to her for a reason.

When she was a young woman, God called her to be a missionary

among Indian children. She loved them, but she felt sorry for the little girls. They were used as slave girls to the old priests in the temples. She wanted them to know about Jesus and how much He loved them. The sad thing was that she didn't look like an Indian. They would never allow her into the temple.

So she took coffee and smeared it all over her face, neck, hands, arms and feet. Then she put on an Indian outfit and wrapped a sari (a scarf) around her head. As she looked at herself in the mirror, a friend said to her, "Amy, isn't God good? You look just like an Indian lady. Your eyes are brown just like theirs."

At that moment she remembered her prayer many, many years before, when she asked God for blue eyes. Well, she spent all her life telling Indian children about Jesus. She even opened her home for them to come and stay with her. She was known as "Amma" (mother) by her family of Indian children.

Sometimes we look in the mirror and don't like what we see. But remember, God knows best and He never makes a mistake.

Amy knew all about this treasure:
I MUST BE HAPPY
THE WAY GOD MADE

ME SOMETHING TO THANK GOD FOR

Dear Lord Jesus, thank You that You have made me just the way that You want me to be. Help me to be happy with the way I look. I'm so glad that You have a special plan for my life. I am here for a reason, just like Amy. Amen.

SOMETHING TO DO

Tonight, take your pillow and blanket, and lie outside on the grass under the stars. Ask your family to join you and sing your favorite songs about Jesus together.

THE WORDLESS BOOK

Dust was everywhere. Dusting cloths, feather dusters and brooms were all in action. Music blaring. Children singing. Grammy beaming from ear to ear. The children had come to help her spring clean her little cottage. Josh picked up a small book that had slipped in behind the bookcase. He was confused. No pictures. No words. Just colors.

Grammy had a twinkle in her eye and introduced them to *The Wordless Book*. As she fanned out the pages in front of the children, they saw a black, red, white, and gold page. The cover was green. "This is called a wordless book," she said, "because it has no words, but tells the most beautiful story ever. It's the Good News in colors.

"Let's start with THE GOLD PAGE. When you see gold you might think of the sun, treasures or stars. But this tells us about God's love. You see, the Bible says that the streets of heaven are paved with gold. The gold page reminds us of heaven, God's home. God loves us and wants us to live with Him forever in heaven.

"The next page is THE BLACK PAGE. Now you might think of a dark night, wizards or Darth Vader from *Star Wars*. It's not a pretty page. But its real meaning here is that we all have a need. Black reminds us of sin and our sinful hearts. You see, we have all sinned and sin does not belong in heaven. Sin is anything that does not please God. It's wanting your own way, lying, stealing, disobeying, cheating and so on. The biggest sin of all is not believing in Jesus.

The Bible says that we have *all* sinned and the punishment is to be separated from God forever. That would be terrible!

"THE RED PAGE gives us hope. I can picture red shoes, a Spiderman top, red roses or even Little Red Riding Hood. But this red page really tells us of God's way. It represents the blood of Jesus that flowed on the cross for you and for me. Because we have sinned, God knew there was nothing we could do to get rid of our sins. "We can try doing all sorts of good things like going to church, reading our Bible or giving to the poor.

"But there is nothing we can do to get ourselves into heaven. So God made a way for us to be forgiven. What a wonderful plan! He

sent His own dear Son, Jesus, from heaven to take the punishment for our sins and to die for us. Remember John 3:16 that says: 'For God so loved the world that He gave His one and only Son, that whoever believes in Him shall not perish but have eternal life.' There is only one way for you and me to be saved from our sins, and that is *God's way*.

"But let's first finish cleaning up the cottage before we look at the rest of the book," Grammy said. "We can finish looking through it later."

If you share this treasure with others it will change their lives:
THE GOOD NEWS IS THAT JESUS SAVES!

SOMETHING TO THANK GOD FOR

Thank You, Lord, that because here was nothing I could do to be good enough for You, You made a plan. You sent Your Son to die for me on a cross so that I can be saved. Thank You for loving me so much. I love You, too. Amen.

SOMETHING TO DO

Draw a cross or cut out a cross on red paper and keep it in your Bible. Let it always remind you how much Jesus loves you and what He did for you on the cross.

WHITER THAN SNOW

The children gathered around Grammy excitedly to hear the last part of the *Wordless Book*. It was family prayer time as usual and everyone took their places in the lounge, and waited for Grammy to continue the story. This was a fascinating little book. Jodi took it in her hands and fanned open the pages again. Gold – black – red – white – green. Cuddled up close beside Grammy, they waited …

"Let's start with THE WHITE PAGE first," Grammy said. "Do you remember the story of the printer's daughter in Germany? Remember how she picked up a piece of paper that read: "For God so loved the world that He gave …" Because of those words on the piece of paper, she said that we should not be afraid of God. We should love Him in return. She was right, Jesus wants all children to love Him and accept Him as their Savior.

"When you think of the color white, you might think of snow, a little lamb or a clean white shirt. But this page tells us about Jesus washing away our sins. The black page taught us that our hearts are black with sin. But, no matter how deep the stains of our sins are, God can remove it. So the color white speaks of washing our hearts clean. Jesus says in His Word that He can make you as clean as freshly fallen snow. Imagine that! When you look at pictures of snow-covered mountains, let it remind you of God's promise to us.

"After receiving Jesus we get a clean, white heart. This brings us to a choice we have to make. We can either accept Jesus into our

hearts or choose not to. If you choose to receive Jesus as your personal Savior, you can pray this prayer:

"Dear Lord Jesus, thank You that You love me so much.
Thank You for dying on the cross for me.
I am sorry for doing wrong and sinful things.
Please come into my heart and forgive all my sins.
I accept You now as my Savior. Thank You, Jesus.
Amen.

"Now for the last color of our book: THE GREEN PAGE. What do you think of when you see green? Have you ever tried to grow a bean in cotton wool? You put the bean in a bowl between wet cottonwool. Water it every day. And then wait and watch! Suddenly you'll see a green shoot and it will start to grow. That's exactly what happens to us after we accept Jesus into our hearts. We start to grow. But we grow God's way. How does that happen? Well let me give you six pointers. You can use your right hand to help you remember them, starting with the little finger and ending up with your thumb.

Then squash your fist together to remind yourself to tell others about the Good News:

* Read your Bible
* Be obedient
* Confess your sins

* Pray
* Meet with other Christians.

Here's a little poem to help you remember:

Study your Bible and obey,
confess your sins and remember to pray.
Meet with other Christians and witness every day,
And you will have the joy of growing God's way.

This treasure will change you
into a child of the King:
GROWING GOD'S WAY IS THE BEST

SOMETHING TO THANK GOD FOR

Thank You, Jesus, that when I asked
You to come into my heart my name
was written in the Book of Life.
As I read the Bible every day,
help me to learn how to
grow up into the person
You want me to be. I
want to be the best
for Jesus!
Amen.

SOMETHING TO DO

Turn to the back
of the book to make your
own wordless book.

SHE'S GONE!

Josh and Jodi were very sad. Their cousin Grace had passed away. Grammy was just the person they wanted to talk to. She told them that as long as they love God, they'll always be only a whisper away from their cousin Grace. They had so many questions to ask. One question was: "What would we do if we lost our mom or our dad?"

So Grammy sat them down and explained how much comfort we can find in the Bible. "It tells us that the Lord also feels sad when one of His people dies, because He loves each one of us. The more we love someone, the more we will miss them when they're gone. How precious it is to know that when we lose a loved one, Jesus is sad for us, too. He knows how much we loved them and how much we will miss them. There will be lots of tears and crying. But remember that you are not alone, because Jesus also cried. He lost a special friend, Lazarus, when He was on earth. The Bible tells us that when Lazarus died, Jesus cried. He has a soft heart, too.

"The Bible also tells us that Jesus decided long ago the day we would be born and the day we would die. And no one can change that. But, the decision where we are going is up to us. It was Grace's time to go home to be with Jesus in heaven."

"Wow, isn't that neat!" exclaimed Josh and Jodi. "To think that Jesus came and took her to His home. But how does that work, Grammy?" asked Jodi.

"Say for instance that you are watching TV and you fall asleep.

Daddy comes and picks you up gently and takes you to your bed. When you wake up you find yourself in your own room and not in the TV lounge. Grace woke up in God's home. You see, Grace's body was the house in which she lived. But her soul – the part that sometimes felt happy or sad, the part that loved her family, friends and Jesus – that part went to be with Jesus. And her body, the lovely house she lived in, was then taken to the funeral home. Then the funeral followed. It was a sad occasion, because we will miss her. But it is also a happy occasion, because we know she is with Jesus. And so we all celebrated her life together."

For a long time Josh and Jodi were quiet and Jodi just stared out of the window. "Grammy, what do you think Grace is doing right now in heaven?"

"I think maybe she is playing with all the other children. Perhaps they are even singing happy songs to Jesus around the throne," Grammy replied.

"But her mom isn't there, so who is going to take care of her?"

"I know that Jesus will take care of her. We just don't have all the answers right now. But one day, when it is our turn to go home and see Jesus, we will have all the answers."

This treasure has a happy ending:
WHEN I DIE I WILL BE WITH JESUS

SOMETHING TO THANK GOD FOR

Thank You, Jesus, that when You come to take me to Your home, I will see You at last. I will hug You and tell You how much I love You. And because You are the King of kings, I am a King's kid! Amen.

SOMETHING TO DO

Write notes to all the people closest to you. Tell them that you love them.

HEAVEN

"Grammy, do you know what heaven will be like?" Josh and Jodi asked. After a moment, Grammy said, "When I was a little girl of three, my mom passed away. And my dad told me she had gone to be with Jesus in heaven. So I used to think that heaven was somewhere behind the clouds and I would often wonder if I would be able to see her face in one of the clouds.

Jodi chipped in: "One of my friends at school told me that she used to write a little note to Jesus and tie it to the end of her kite string. Then she would lie on the grass and let go of her kite, watching it go up and up and up. And she wondered when Jesus would get it." Grammy continued, "But let's see what the Bible says heaven is really like: Heaven is a happy place. When you arrive at the gates made of pearl, God will be there on His throne and Jesus beside Him, waiting to welcome you home. Then there's a book called the Lamb's Book of Life. It will be opened. The moment we received Jesus as our Savior, our names were written in that Book. Is your name in that Book?

"We will also see our family and friends that have gone to heaven before us and also thousands and thousands of angels. Maybe you'll even play with other children and sing songs of praise to Jesus!

"And guess what? No church or Sunday school. Why? Because God will be right there to worship! We definitely won't just play harps and sit on clouds. God has a plan for all of us when we get there. I'm so excited to hear that no one will die again. We will never be sad or sick or even cry because God will wipe all our tears away. We will never sin again because the devil won't be there to tempt us to do wrong. God will throw him

into an eternal fire called hell and get rid of him forever.

"I think heaven will be bright and beautiful. The streets will be of glittering gold where we'll walk and dance and sing for joy to Jesus! Can you imagine walls and floors full of sparkling jewels like jasper, emerald and sapphire? Well that's what we'll see! And what's more we'll see 12 gates of precious pearls, just like the string of pearls your mommy sometimes wears.

"In heaven you will never ever be afraid of the dark. We won't need candles or a sun or a moon. You see, Jesus is the brightest light you can ever imagine and He will light up all of heaven. It will be better than any firework display!

"Guess what? Jesus is the best Gardener ever because He has planted a tree of life in heaven. It's a wonderful tree that grows different fruit every month. Imagine that!

"You're probably wondering where we will live? Well, God is busy preparing a room for each one of us in His beautiful house. And God is the best Designer, Builder and Architect ever. Can you imagine how busy He must be and all the excitement up there as He gets it ready for us?

"Jesus says He's coming back soon in the clouds to fetch us. He longs for us to come home and be with Him forever. What a wonderful day that will be! We will live happily ever after. Aren't you looking forward to heaven? I know I am!"

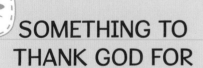
This treasure is the most beautiful treasure of all:
HEAVEN IS A WONDERFUL PLACE

SOMETHING TO THANK GOD FOR

Thank You, Jesus, that You are busy getting a room ready for me in Your house. I can't wait to see You. Help me to tell others about You in the meantime so that they will also be with me in heaven one day. It will be so amazing if my whole family is there with me!
Amen.

SOMETHING TO DO

Lie on your back and look up at the clouds. Just imagine how beautiful it must be up there in heaven.

TREASURES FOR YOUR TREASURE CHEST

GOD IS A GOD OF MIRACLES

JESUS FORGIVES

GOD WILL NEVER LEAVE ME

GOD CAN USE EVEN ME

JESUS WANTS ME TO BELONG TO HIM

GROWING GOD'S WAY IS THE BEST

GOD WANTS US TO ALWAYS OWN UP

JESUS WANTS TO LIVE IN MY HEART

I AM SPECIAL

I WILL BE KIND TO OTHERS

JESUS LOVES ME

I WILL TELL OTHERS ABOUT JESUS

GOD WILL ALWAYS HELP ME

GOD HELPS ME TO MAKE GOOD CHOICES

GOD WANTS ME TO OBEY MY PARENTS

JESUS IS PLEASED WHEN I TELL THE TRUTH

WHEN I DIE I WILL BE WITH JESUS

I MUST REMEMBER TO ALWAYS SAY "THANK YOU"

GOD HEARS AND ANSWERS PRAYER

I MUST BE HAPPY THE WAY GOD MADE ME

I CAN TALK TO JESUS EVERY DAY

HEAVEN IS A WONDERFUL PLACE

THE GOOD NEWS IS THAT JESUS SAVES

MY WORDLESS BOOK

 GOLD God loves us and wants us to live forever with Him in heaven.

"If I go and prepare a place for you, I will come back and take you to be with Me that you also may be where I am."

John 14:3

 BLACK We have all sinned and sin separates us from God.

For all have sinned and fall short of the glory of God.

Romans 3:23

 RED God sent His own Son, Jesus Christ, to die on the cross so that we can be saved.

The blood of Jesus His Son cleanses us from all sin.

1 John 1:7

 WHITE Jesus washes our sins away and makes our hearts clean.

Cleanse me with hyssop, and I will be clean; wash me, and I will be whiter than snow.

Psalm 51:7

 GREEN When Jesus lives in our hearts we start to grow and become what He wants us to be.

Grow in the grace and knowledge of our Lord and Savior Jesus Christ.

2 Peter 3:18

INSTRUCTIONS

Cut along the dotted lines and staple the book together as indicated. You now have your own wordless book to share with others!

PLACE THE PAGES ON TOP OF EACH OTHER IN THE FOLLOWING ORDER

ALIGN YOUR PAGES NEATLY ON TOP OF EACH OTHER AND STAPLE THEM TOGETHER TO FORM A WORDLESS BOOK

CUT ALONG THE LINE

CUT ALONG THE LINE TO THE END OF THE PAGE

CUT ALONG THE LINE TO THE END OF THE PAGE

CUT ALONG THE LINE TO THE END OF THE PAGE

CUT ALONG THE LINE TO THE END OF THE PAGE